Investigate

Teeth

Charlotte Guillain

Heinemann
LIBRARY

www.heinemann.co.uk/library
Visit our website to find out more information about Heinemann Library books.

To order:
☎ Phone 44 (0) 1865 888066

📄 Send a fax to 44 (0) 1865 314091

💻 Visit the Heinemann Bookshop at www.heinemann.co.uk/library to browse our catalogue and order online.

Heinemann Library is an imprint of Pearson Education Limited, a company incorporated in England and Wales having its registered office at Edinburgh Gate, Harlow, Essex, CM20 2JE – Registered company number: 00872828

Heinemann is a registered trademark of Pearson Education Ltd.
Text © Pearson Education Limited 2008
First published in hardback in 2008
Paperback edition first published in 2009

Edited by Sarah Shannon, Catherine Clarke, and Laura Knowles
Designed by Joanna Hinton-Malivoire, Victoria Bevan, and Hart McLeod
Picture research by Liz Alexander
Production by Duncan Gilbert
Originated by Chroma Graphics (Overseas) Pte. Ltd
Printed and bound in China by Leo Paper Group

ISBN 978 0 431932 70 5 (hardback)
12 11 10 09 08
10 9 8 7 6 5 4 3 2 1

ISBN 978 0 431932 89 7 (paperback)
13 12 11 10 09
10 9 8 7 6 5 4 3 2 1

British Library Cataloguing in Publication Data
Guillain, Charlotte
  Teeth. - (Investigate)
  573.3'56
BA full catalogue record for this book is available from the British Library.

Acknowledgements
We would like to thank the following for permission to reproduce photographs: ©Alamy pp. **6** (Images of Africa Photobank), **7** (Bryan & Cherry Alexander Photography), **11** (BRUCE COLEMAN INC.), **13** (Danita Delimont), **25** (ACE STOCK LIMITED), **27** (Premaphotos), **29** (JUPITERIMAGES/BananaStock); ©Corbis pp. **9** (Paul A. Souders), **21** (Lucidio Studio, Inc.); ©Dorling Kindersley p. **17** (Colin Keates/Courtesy of the Natural History Museum, London); ©FLPA pp. **5** (Richard Du Toit/Minden Pictures), **15** (NORBERT WU/Minden Pictures), **18** (Terry Whittaker); ©Getty Images pp. **8** (Iconica), **24** (Digital Vision), **26** (Michael Rosenfeld); ©naturepl.com p. **14** (Francois Savigny); ©Pearson Education Ltd. p. **23** (Tudor Photography. 2007), ©Photolibrary pp. **4** (Stockbyte), **10** (Stan Osolinski), **19** (Pacific Stock), **28** (PhotoAlto/Eric Audras).

Cover photograph of face of happy boy smiling reproduced with permission of ©DK Stock (Christina Kennedy).

Every effort has been made to contact copyright holders of material reproduced in this book. Any omissions will be rectified in subsequent printings if notice is given to the publishers.

Contents

Some words are shown in bold, **like this**. You can find out what they mean by looking in the glossary.

Teeth for eating

People need teeth for eating. We need to eat food to stay alive and to grow. Our teeth break up food so we can swallow it.

Many animals also have teeth. Animals use their teeth to eat with too. Birds do not have teeth. They use their hard beaks to break up food.

This zebra is showing off its teeth and gums!

Some animals use their teeth as tools. They use them:
- ➠ to break things
- ➠ to carry things
- ➠ to fight other animals.

⬇ An elephant's tusks are teeth. An elephant uses its tusks for many things, such as digging up roots to eat and fighting.

tusk

Male walruses fight each other with their tusks.

A walrus also has tusks. A walrus uses its tusks to pull itself out of the water on to land. It also uses its tusks to break breathing holes in the ice when it is under water.

7

Incisors

People have different types of teeth. They are called **incisors**, **canines**, and **molars**. All these teeth work in different ways to help us eat.

Incisors are used to bite and cut food. Incisors are sharp and are at the front of the mouth.

Q Which animal has these incisors?

CLUES

- These incisors are used for biting hard things such as wood.

- These incisors are very strong.

9

A These teeth are a beaver's incisors. The beaver uses them to cut down trees and eat the tree bark. A beaver's incisors have a hard outer covering that stays strong and sharp.

Some animals have incisors that do not stop growing. These animals use their incisors to bite food over and over again. This is called **gnawing**. It wears down the teeth so they do not grow too long.

Canines

People have **canines** on either side of their **incisors**.
Canines are pointed teeth. We use them to grip and
tear up the food we eat.

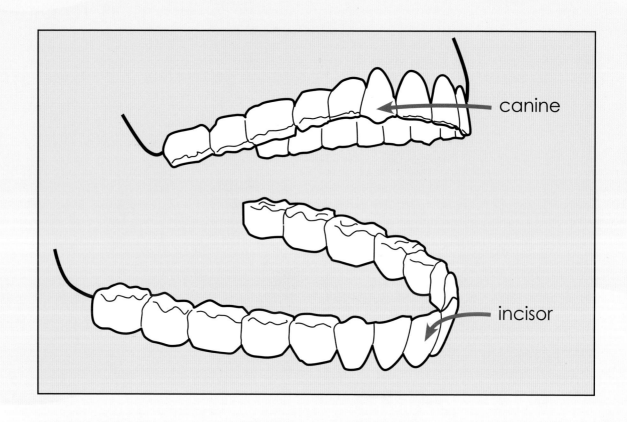

canine

incisor

? CLUES

- This animal only eats meat.

- This animal has orange and black striped fur.

A These teeth are a tiger's canines. Tigers use their canine teeth to tear up the meat they eat.

Dogs also have very sharp canine teeth. Another name for a dog is a canine.

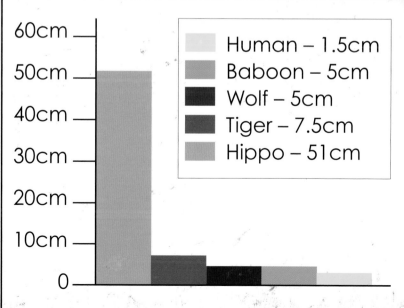

Human – 1.5cm
Baboon – 5cm
Wolf – 5cm
Tiger – 7.5cm
Hippo – 51cm

This bar chart compares the lengths of different canine teeth. Which animal in this chart has the longest canines?

Molars

People have **molars** at the back of their mouth. Molars are large and flat. We use them to chew and grind our food into pieces.

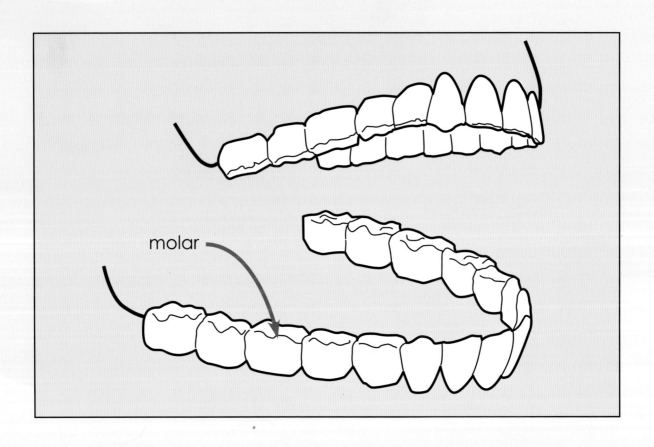

molar

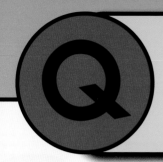 Most animals have molars to chew their food. This skull belongs to an animal with many strong molars. What sort of food does it eat?

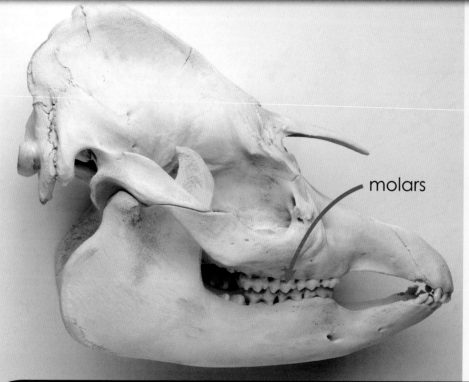

molars

 CLUE

- What type of food needs grinding and crushing?

A Tapirs eat leaves, tree bark, flowers and fruit. They do not eat meat.

A young South American Tapir. Animals that do not eat meat are called **herbivores**.

Some animals, such as elephants and manatees, have special molars. The molars at the front of the mouth get worn down when the animal eats. The front molars fall out and the molars at the back of the mouth move forwards. Then new teeth grow at the back.

What is inside a tooth?

Teeth grow out of the bones in the jaw. The part of the tooth that we can see is covered in **enamel**. Enamel is very hard. Enamel is a thin coating that protects the tooth.

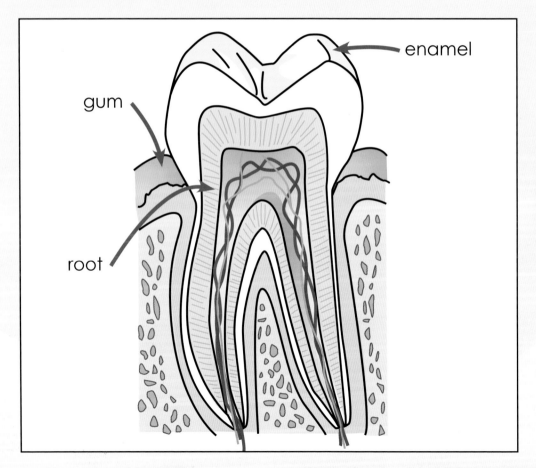

enamel

gum

root

This diagram shows the inside of a tooth.

What happens if there is a hole in the enamel of a tooth?

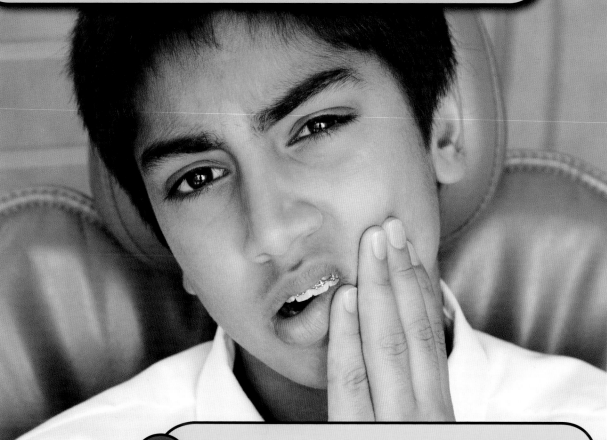

? **CLUE**

- It hurts when you eat.

A If there is a hole in the enamel on a tooth we get toothache. The hole is called a **cavity**. Cavities form because of **tooth decay**.

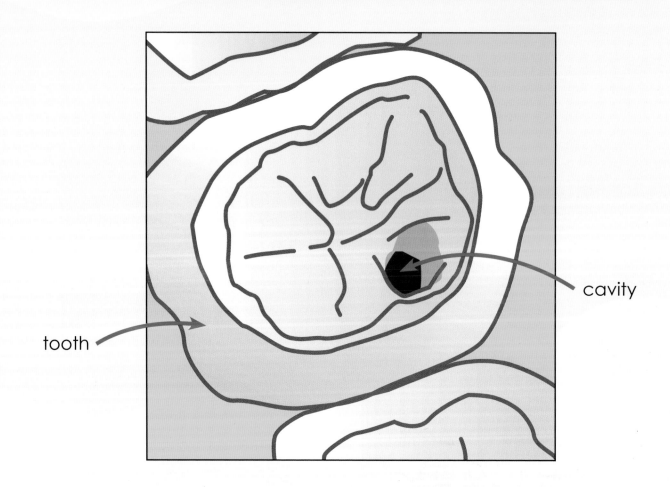

cavity

tooth

Sugar makes teeth decay. Sugar can stick to teeth and make something called **plaque**. It makes holes in your teeth. This is tooth decay.

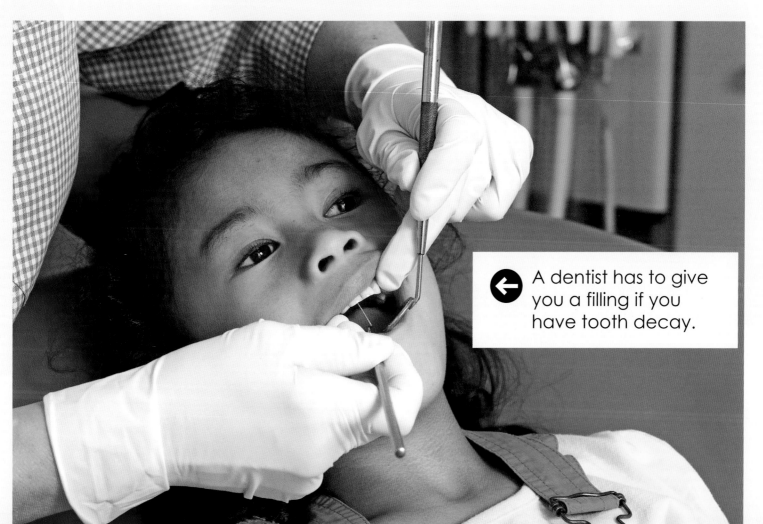

A dentist has to give you a filling if you have tooth decay.

Looking after teeth

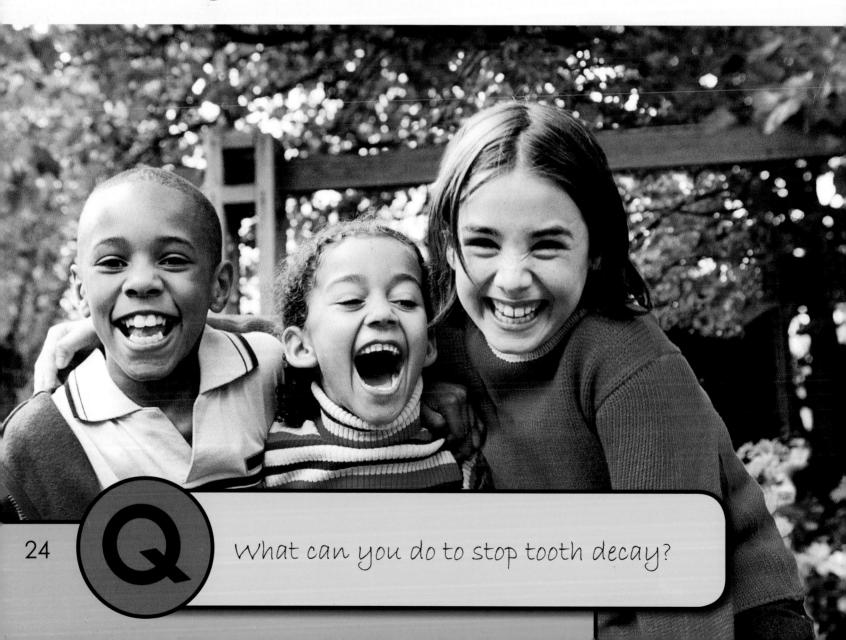

Q What can you do to stop tooth decay?

?

CLUE

• What can you do to look after your teeth?

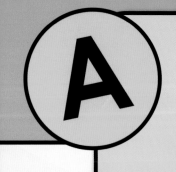

A We can stop **tooth decay** by brushing our teeth twice a day and visiting the dentist regularly. We can also eat healthy food that does not hurt our teeth. Fruit and vegetables are good for our teeth because they do not have too much sugar. Sweets and sugary drinks are bad for our teeth.

These foods contain calcium that keeps our teeth strong.

Animal teeth stay healthy in different ways:

➡ Some animals' teeth keep growing. This means they always have strong new teeth to eat with.

➡ Some crocodiles keep their teeth clean by using a helper. They let birds pick the food off their teeth.

People have two sets of teeth. Our first set of teeth are called **milk teeth**. They usually fall out when we are about five or six years old. The new, big teeth are called **permanent teeth**.

We need our teeth to eat well and stay healthy. We cannot replace our permanent teeth, so we need to look after them.

Clean your teeth at least twice a day and always before you go to bed.

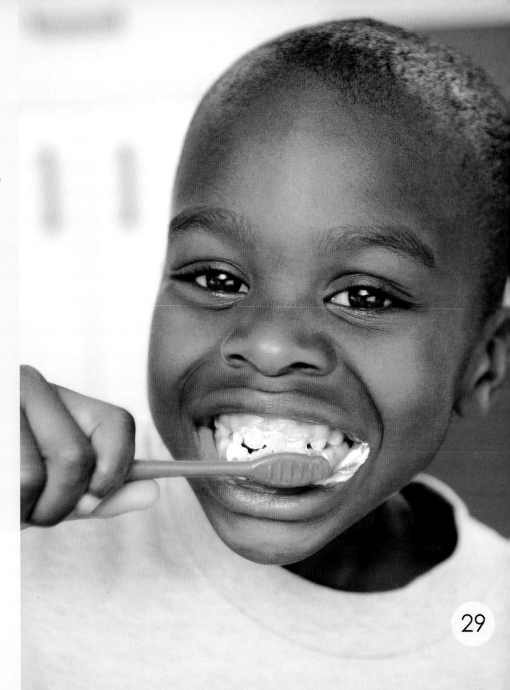

Checklist

People have **milk teeth** and later grow **permanent teeth**.

People have three types of teeth:
➠ **incisors**
➠ **canines**
➠ **molars**.

Different animals have different types of teeth.

Birds have no teeth.

Glossary

canines sharp teeth for gripping and tearing food

cavity hole in a tooth caused by decay

enamel thin, hard coating on the outside of a tooth

herbivore animal that only eats plants

gnaw to bite at something over and over

incisors teeth for biting and cutting food

milk teeth first teeth that young children have

molars   teeth to crush and grind food

permanent teeth adult teeth that replace milk teeth

plaque layer that forms on teeth after eating

tooth decay damage caused to teeth that are not cleaned properly

Index